BOA
EDITIONS
LIMITED

CABATO SENTORA

Poems by
Ray Gonzalez

BOA Editions, Ltd. ⁓ Rochester, NY ⁓ 1999

LC #: 98–72192
ISBN: 1–880238–70–5 paper

First Edition
99 00 01 02 7 6 5 4 3 2 1

Publications by BOA Editions, Ltd.—
a not-for-profit corporation under section 501 (c) (3)
of the United States Internal Revenue Code—
are made possible with the assistance of grants from
the Literature Program of the New York State Council on the Arts,
the Literature Program of the National Endowment for the Arts,
the Lannan Foundation, the Sonia Raiziss Giop Charitable Foundation,
the Eric Mathieu King Fund of The Academy of American Poets,
as well as from the Mary S. Mulligan Charitable Trust,
the County of Monroe, NY,
and from many individual supporters.

Cover Design: Nancy David
Typesetting: Richard Foerster
Manufacturing: McNaughton & Gunn, Lithographers
BOA Logo: Mirko

BOA Editions, Ltd.
Richard Garth, Chair
A. Poulin, Jr., President & Founder (1976–1996)
260 East Avenue
Rochester, NY 14604

This book is for the silence of my father and my grandfathers.
For the language of their silence.

Contents

IV. The Poor Angel

V. Sentora

I
Cabato

Calling the White Donkey

I called the white donkey that hurt my left shoulder
the last time it appeared, ramming me
with its ivory head, cracking my back
to relieve me of worry and hope.
I called the white donkey,
surprised at the sound of my voice.
I was scared, wondering if the white head
would give me its donkey brain,
snowy matter dripping into my ears
like the horse of the first man who fell off,
the mind of the donkey teaching me about
desire, the moan, white hair
on the back of my head that warns me.

I called the donkey.
It came slowly toward me,
huge ears shaking with growing fury,
the smell of its breath turning the air white,
a greed wanting to bite into the white apple
I have carried in my throat since I was a boy.
I faced the donkey, watched
its gait become a shuffle of possession,
shaking its head as it stopped to
root its dirty hooves in the ground.

I stepped back and clicked my fingers.
It would not come closer, its snort
commanding I listen as it farted.
I walked away and did not know it was I
who yearned for labor of the ass.
It came so close before letting me know
the animal I summoned couldn't remove
the white scar from my heart,
a blind life I lived for good.

Under the Freeway in El Paso

I hear streets light up
with secret weeping,

wish I could really hear it,
be given the owl

and the route of veins
pulsing under the freeway

where the house of my birth
stands and decays.

Strangers have lived there
for the last thirty-eight years.

I have wanted to knock on the door
and breathe inside the house.

Someone wants me
to disguise myself as a street,

a traffic signal or a dark alley,
the imploded house across

from the last residence
of the ghost who follows me inside.

Someone wants me to thrive,
surpass the disappearance

of my father, my dead grandfathers,
my missing uncle, my cousins

who won't speak to me because
I come from the house of candles,

the room of saints, the wall of glowing
crucifixes that break the arms

of those who don't believe,
who curse the smoke

and blow it toward me,
the blankets I found inside

shattered rooms under
the freshly built freeway.

I went crazy with hope there,
restless as the prisoner

who fell down the hill,
impaled himself on yucca

and the turnpike of America,
the pointed staff of the priest.

I am the man who ate
the catacombs of honey,

raised my lips to the wiping hands
that took care of me inside the house,

gave me sweetness of prayer,
the stranger waiting for my return,

so he could light the candles
that didn't melt in the years of the passenger.

Confessional

Here is the confessor
with his metal cross
pressed to his forehead,
throat of pure voices
stumbling over prayer.
How he wishes he could
grasp the rosary,
root the beads into smoke
under enormous church floors,
roll them into marbles
the size of his testicles,
as they fold under him,
trying to disappear from the cold.
He stands from genuflection
like a silent dancer.

Take a candle.
Light it.
Take a mouth not making sound.
A mouth of night that
hasn't answered in years.
When the dead nun rises
out of the confessional,
take your memory of her.
She is the first-grade teacher
who beat you years ago,
blood running down your forehead
as a trickle the priest forgot to bless.

Sit in the middle
of the empty, black church.
Smell the air of sinners
and those who don't cry.

Then, in a voice that doesn't lie,
a voice with a dust of holy water—
bless the ghost, bless the water.

Suddenly, I Remember the Place

Loud thunder of the white guitar decides how far
we recall the danger of telling too many tales
to the black hand of the draped saint,
the statue in the garden overgrown with dry roses,
salt cedars, the deep grotto of spreading leaves.
Visiting loyal worshipers not knowing the saint
in the grotto has been covered for years—
actually a woman condemned to die in the sun
for having too much strength—the mistaken figure
of a male saint buried under her, worms
and rotting earth strong under the statue.

The sanctuary with the shriveled mummy in the glass
belongs to the Franciscans who never came out
when we visited, a walled-in shrine in a neighborhood
that hid the secret of petrified stone and shells,
angry brothers hooded in brown cloth, the ropes
around their waists tighter than the black branches
that hovered over my head when I let go of my mother's
hand to get a good look at the face of the mummy.

I don't recall how long it looked back at me,
before it disintegrated into the nightmare I have
several times a year. My mother insisted I come see
the grotto for myself, wanting me to pay for my sins
of hitting my sisters, lying to her, hiding behind
the house when my father searched for me,
his leather belt blistering my back with the same
bony peaks I saw on the shrouded saint.

Loud thunder of the white guitar
on my tattooed hand, a pattern I bought from
a gum wrapper to print on my wrist, pretend
I could run from the thick vines of the saint—
terror and the guilt of boys among the circle

of hooded men asking for gifts, an exposed genital
from the punished youth who belonged
to the blind gathering of the faithful.

The boy never questioned the grotto, never asked
why the sky turned black each time they visited
the suffocating armpit of incense, glass,
black hoods, sandaled feet, and the red eyes
of the monk who took the boy with a cold hand,
stood him before the enclosed body, forced him
to confess beyond the dimensions of shattered glass.

Vista Across a Tree

Start with the secret source of those
who taught you how to write and sing.
Despair over the unreachable extension
of things you were told you could possess.

Continue with the flag of doubt
over the fields of finely cut grass moving
into memory of a cold, stone floor,
the overburdened arms of the cottonwood.

Vista with crosses and people entering the arches,
overpowering smoke of incense from troubled altars.
When you leave the church each time,
you inherit a piece of paper to write on.

You do not know it.
You never carry the pages with you.
They are hidden in the well where your cousin fell
and drowned, a puzzle of bones and candy skulls

of the holiday intended to make fun
of the crying wolves, the beekeepers,
mounds of *masa* turning yellow on the table,
their puffy nipples of salt oozing onto plates of tomatoes

cut to please you, feed you as a son of the kitchen,
stinging taste of mescal heaving your broken stomach
as the one who shared his tongue
with men who could not stay quiet.

Share this with those who taught you.
They have written their books of greed, books of knives,
books of bandannas and torn jeans, the list
of women's names they kept.

Let them have their books.
You have one and it is turning yellow.
Keep the mask of asking on the back of your head.
You don't have to wear it on your face

until laughter abolishes masks.
Forget masks.
They don't exist.
They are coloring books for the dead.

If a trail of ants outside your house condemns you,
rid yourself of every pitcher of water.
Friends without water.
Vista of a tree fallen in the lightning strike.

The code of clay breaks in the library.
It is missing pieces you stole when you began
your vocabularies, set down words on paper
from churches you hated to enter.

Your friend's mother lived in the barrios of El Paso,
a singer and guitarist with heat in her stomach,
sharpness of her breasts that enveloped her sons,
tossed them into the blinding coil of the desert,
so they could wipe the dust off their blackened feet.

Fingerprints flashing in your eyes
during the rare July storm.
If you could explain this to your friends,
you would not be friends.

If they ask you about guacamole on lettuce leaves,
tell them the salad comes from two kinds of greed.
If they show you their poems of doubt,
announce the letters to the code of clay

given to you by your mother.
It is the myth of the dying coyote
poisoned by the naughty boys, lies
of the hungry wanting what you left on your plate,

the leather strap across your back,
vista of the tree in the hands
of the father with the belt
who has nothing to do with this.

Cabato

Cabato—*the art of tying sticks together with brown twine to make a secret symbol only the maker knows.*

I tie eight sticks together, make sure
they look like the first star that fell at my feet.
The brown twine is tight, finished,
wound around the middle of the long,
smooth bamboo sticks.
It is not a star, but a falling diamond,
the closest pyramid that rose near
San Luis Potosí where my grandmother was born.

I make my cabato.
It has sixteen points resembling the cage of sorrows,
two feet long at its widest point,
a twisted wreath for those who want me
to tell them what it means.

I twirl my cabato in my hands,
a bamboo forest eliminated when
the first people found my grandmother,
gave her the will to live, letting members
of her family they didn't kill, flee.

I hang my cabato on the wall, stiff vine
of what I always wanted to make.
The sticks remain.
The mutated star will dry into the wall
until the day I die.

I touch my cabato.
No one knows what I think
when I make sure the twine is secure,

the geometrical cross I have made a part
of the same tool invented by the first man
who tied anything together.

Meditation at Chamberino

When Juan de Oñate came this way
his men died of thirst following the river.
They had no church as they entered El Jornado del Muerto.
The old tower stands here, making a difference in the sun,
pecked by pigeons that have shit on the walls for hundreds of years.

When the masked executioner drew his sword,
the traitor begged Juan to let him back into the army—
the conquistadores dying one by one, this small village
rising out of lava rocks that survived the dry river,
forced the men to leave a large cross in the dirt.

*

When I drove through this valley road, no one remembered me,
no one knew I hit an old dog one night on this curve,
saw it leap in agony across the irrigation canal,
its howls taking me into the adobe walls behind the church.
Years later, finding the ruins about to be rebuilt
where I hid my shame, now polished and new.
Kneeling inside the church, there is the danger I have not given enough.

Rising to make the sign of the cross, I feel a burning in my side.
I know the sword of the one who passed through here
is the knife my father used when he was in high school,
running with an early gang before the years of the mad cities and guns,
far from this sanctuary where I sharpen his blade.

*

First bead on the rosary for guilt.
Second black bead for the dead man in the tower.
Third prayer for the incense that almost
killed me when I went to mass with my father,
the only time he took me, carrying me out when the priest swung

the pot with smoke, the poison of the dry river, the silence between us
having to pass through the valley to get to this church,
the place where I will return to and hide, someday.

Fourth black ball
for the wrong things I have told him.
Fifth hard pebble

for the marks on my back.
Sixth bead
for the way I was able to breathe, again.

The seventh fingered rosary knot
for the space in this falling chamber
where I mark my forehead with the ash of the soul,

confessing justice has nothing to do
with the wounded man, spoiled holy water
invisible above my head,

creaks on the boarded stairs leading to the tower where blood
is the mark of the scout who gave Juan de Oñate hope
when he rose from his shallow grave and moaned,

his hair standing on his head, white face glowing
through the armor, his skin illuminating the river,
leading them away from the broken doors,

and the altar that has not burned
four hundred years after men and horses sank
into red soil on the way to their whispering end.

Pancho Villa Invites My Grandfather
to the Revolution, Mexico, 1914

He offers Bonifacio a pistol and a woman,
promises of land to fight the Federales,
my grandfather at fourteen never seeing the blood
of change before the battle for the border town,
fear growing inside his pounding heart.
Villa invites my grandfather to sit and eat with him,
stacks of warm tortillas, frijoles, and jalapeños
offered to the volunteers as the reward for liberation.
Bonifacio eats in silence, looks timidly at the great hero,
wonders if this will be his last meal,
if he can kill for the first time.

Villa rises from the table, toasts the young boys
with tequila, laughs because many will die without
knowing how many of their mothers, wives,
and sisters his men will take in the name of freedom.
Bonifacio stands with his *compañeros*,
drinks the tequila and is told to leave.
He is given an old rifle and a few bullets,
told where to gather for the assault.

He never sees Villa again, only fires his rifle
four times before the battle is over.
He doesn't shoot anyone, stares at the fourteen
Federales who are lined up and executed,
the five whose heads are cut off.
Dropping his rifle behind a burning wagon,
Bonifacio runs toward the river where Julia,
my grandmother, waits in El Paso.
He tries to cross at nightfall,
hears the cries of men in the water.

He clings to the bottom of the low, wooden bridge,
thinks of his meal with Villa.
Three bodies float by as gunshots flash behind him,
horses splashing violently downstream.
Bonifacio closes his eyes to the dream he had last night,
where they served him his head on a wooden plate,
set it on a table for the laughing men
who occupied Bonifacio's town.

My grandfather dreamed this ten years before
the hero was gunned down, the assassins molding
the death mask of Pancho Villa, cutting off his head,
only to lose it somewhere between Chihuahua
and the bridge where Bonifacio crossed to meet Julia,
black waters of the Rio Grande foaming
toward the other side of the world.

Llaga

Llaga line of delicate gourds installed
behind my ear before I was born.

Llaga lord of the soft doubt and mistaken birthmark
of four tiny black moles on my right wrist.

Llaga markers pointing to the arm of fate,
removing the legend from where it lies.

Llaga fish stay in the water as I drink from the baptismal chamber.
I have no sense of their fury or schools of millions.

Forty-five years after my Llaga birth, a comet the size of a mountain
hurls toward Jupiter, about to explode with what we have never seen,

changing the Llaga warrior into the Llaga blind man.
I won't deceive you.

I got off the speeding comet years ago, inherited a blue larynx
from the family of Llaga—the only one named after me—

doubting my memory of the future,
how those cracked gourds finally reached me.

I can't speak without removing that blue throat from my body,
can't introduce you to Llaga without asking you to remove

your voice so I can examine it, try it on before
the open boats where Llaga died are closed to us.

Llaga lines on our precious maps.
Once, I prayed with open hands,

sucked on my swollen fingers to make sure
my instincts were sincere.

Breastbone

*In Mexico, a young boy is bitten by a snake and lies
paralyzed for months. His grandfather, a shaman, predicts
that if he lives he will become a great leader.*

He lives and becomes Llaga, the blind man
who sees through his nipples.
He wears no shirt, his bare chest adorned
with beads from broken beer bottles.
He has polished them, hung them around his neck,
brown glass reflecting what he can't see,
hiding him from the people who trust him for advice.

His nipples are dark and wrinkled.
They never rise or harden.
They must stay close to his heart,
so he can remind those around him
his eyes were the nests of the rattler that bit him,
the oval entrances to their dying town.
His chest is turning gray.
Thin hair on it surrounds his eyes.
When he bathes in the river,
he can see under the water.

No one in the town knows the name Llaga.
He tells no one, but the name is there.
It can be found in the thought that blinks
inside the first stranger to approach him.
Llaga does not reveal many things.
His drum is torn.
He can't be described without his white hair
woven around his neck, hanging
between his shoulder blades like the rope
the strangers tried to hang him with,
years ago, before he discovered
he could see through his nipples.

The young boy survived.
He could see.
He opened his eyes.
The fresh strips of snake meat hung,
dripping a white liquid on the pole.
Years had not passed.
It was only a moment
in the life of the fang.

Mexican

There was an eagle high above the painted sorrow.

How do you know what this means?

I spell like the monkey of anger.

Can you follow the flute as it crashes into the well of ruins?

There was a trail cut into the red mountain
where my father stayed.
He dwelled there without anger or disease.
He took women in, ate out
of clean bowls and cut his hair with a torch,
made me obey him, showed me
how to cut my own hair.
He never spoke about his lies or myths,
lived as if the world understood him.
He walked out one day.
I did not follow.

How can you forgive the belly button?

I ate the flesh from the bone.
I traced his outline in the dirt and stood back.

Can you follow him and still be his son?

There was an eagle high above the painted chair.

How many sons have sat there?

I saw a fire in the desert and watched it spread.
No one put it out and it covered the world.
The smoke entered our house and removed my sins.
There was an eagle in the black cloud of smoke.

I thought I saw it, but I could have been wrong.
I have been teaching my son who was never born.

A man killed a snake with his bare feet.

How did he know the fang belonged to him?

There was a man cutting the bite on his leg with a knife.
He spit the poison at my feet.
I held onto his shoulders and sweating head.
I thought I knew who he was, but he disappeared.
He told me about the oncoming jungle
and took the first train.

Did he know where the tracks were going?

He knew how to jump from the moving train.

When did he get off?

He was found in the boxcar full of
suffocated men and women.
He was the only one alive.

Did he get rid of the snake poison?

I can't answer what has not touched me
because I grew up without a father.
He entered walls in silence and dwelled there.
His black hair turned white, then back to black.
His body was fat, then thin.
He belted me hard so I could see,
gave me money, food, the power
to silence his sins in me.

I grew older thinking the eagle fell between father and son.
I had no choice, but died without a father.
He was a burial mound, the deep grave of the eagle,
a place neither my father nor I have seen,

because we are not sons of snakebitten men
digging themselves out of the ground.

How do you know this is true?

I can retell this without staring at the floor.
If I look up on the wall, I will see the largest,
whitest moth I have ever seen.

⌣

The Healing Leaves

When my legs and arms ached
with growing pains as a boy,
my grandmother pulled out
her bottle of rubbing alcohol,
a muddy-brown oil of soaking leaves.
Strong smell of healing rose
when she opened the green bottle,
tipped it in her large palms,
rubbed me down with the leaves,
black shreds of wet skin,
shining pieces of strong branches.

Overpowering plants fermented
in a bottle that carried a dark swamp,
a fire that cured me as hot hands traced
leaves across my trembling arms,
covered my legs like a small animal
wrapping itself around the smoking trees.
When my legs and arms ached,
I went into the cloud of curing,
fumes of touch transforming my pain
into a hidden bone of passage,
a throat-clearing odor that burned me
with secrets I do not say.

Explain

Once in a while God takes poetry away from me.
—Adelia Prado

When I can't speak, the guitar of my dead brother
announces a longing for what should have been,
what could have kept the river farther from our home.

When I can't talk, the maraca of the old man
comes down the street,
rattling for all of us to get up.

It is early,
we fear the rain.
The first lightning of dawn hasn't hit.

When I can't explain,
the old man and his noise love me, the steady beat
telling me I should have been born mute

without tongue or hands, with the fat,
small feet of men in my family,
slow movement where there is nothing to say.

When I can't speak,
the mud oven by the house smokes for those
whose hunger explains whispering words.

When I can't speak,
I reveal what is hidden in the black cellar
I entered as a boy, pushed

the heavy, wooden door to fall into
a pile of old, grease-stained clothes
smelling of the men who did talk,

the ones I recall the instant of my birth,
how they stood around the bed,
congratulated my mother with a language,

a habit I have been sounding since,
the smell of their clothes suffocating me
out of the cellar,

releasing what they said
into the peace
of the backyard air.

Yaqui Poems from Hidden Ancestors

Palo Seco

> Palo Seco—*dry stick*—*Yaqui origin myth that a stick will*
> *tap-tap-tap as a sign of good things to come.*

I tap my stick on a rock.
Nothing happens when I open my eyes.
I do not feel different.
Has someone told the lie they fished out
of the cold campfire?
Have I done it wrong?
I found the stick on one of my walks,
thought I saw a streak of red
in the long, brown knob of it.
I can't recall because I heard sounds
that followed me home.

I tap my stick on the ground.
It slips out of my hand and falls.
I walk away because the cells
in my body have broken through
the fat and hardness of doubt,
settled on the other side of
a hidden story I recently found was true—
a stick tapped for the family.

They prosper in another land,
drink from a different river,
repeat the circular tapping,
grabbing every corner of fortune
they can find in the dry canals
of San Luis Potosí.
They fight wars and take prisoners
to serve, seduce, and bear them
children with twisted mouths of

those who have taken too much.
The stick taps for them.

There is one stick in each of my legs,
sticks that have tapped for the family.
They have held me up, walked me
with careful terror toward the cripple
leaning against the rocks.
He is the only one the family
left behind when they fled.

I leave the sticks alone.
When the family arrives,
I leave sticks alone,
stop making umbilical cords
out of their sticks.
When the family arrives,
I wait for the tap-tap-tap
of an ear as it picks up
the sound of the blind asking
which town, which heat,
which long cane will tremble
like the drummer who died?

Chictura

> Chictura—*Yaqui condition of disorientation*

Muffled cries of discovering the lost particles
have something to do with losing my way
through the *ocotillo, mimosa,* salt cedar,
and *cholla* to find that the cuts and holes of a spiced prayer
have been married to my skin for years.

Fever was not my dance.
It was my swollen foot that came toward my brain
at the age of five when I fell off the red wagon,
cried in front of boys I didn't know,

was carried into the house by my uncle,
so I could faint and repeat the pattern—
Chictura, llorón, stealing attention in the chain
of events that led to being outcast by relatives,
who hated the tears of pain as much as they hated
the silence of the visiting angel who insulted them.

The funny way the mind develops a sanctuary for heaven,
a hole in the ground where the pigs are slaughtered
to feed the workers, where the mana cooked her beans,
dropped a secret bead into the pot, where I first ate
a meal without help, listened to them talk about
the powers of biting into the wrong bean, coming out
on the other side of the mountain as a crossed man.

I don't know when it stopped spinning,
but the top with feathers on it whirled across the floor,
gaining speed to collect the thoughts of every child
who stood around it and watched it twirl,
hoping it would stop and point at them.
They would be the ones to take it home,
take the top apart, pull the feathers off
and tear the nail from the bottom.
Opening the metal top to find nothing inside,
this intrusion of space left me cursed because
I was the one who got to take the top.

Sabio (Yaqui Wise Man)

The Sabio came to see me.
He got tired of waiting for me to go to him.
He arrived as a beautiful shape I mistook
for a blister on my finger.
He shed my skin and borrowed the sweat
from my palm to call his body into the room.

The *Sabio* destroyed me when he sat
on the edge of my bed, whispered that
I was the son who was left behind,
who never knew the embryo stored
in the clay jar was the brother who made it
into the mountains, before falling out
of his dying mother to change the number
of males who made it across.

The *Sabio* blessed me with the shriveled
skull of an iguana, waved the shiny fang
of a rattler over both my arms.
I reached into my humming testicles
and got out of the bed to make him disappear,
because the man who reaches down
is the man who is able to forgive anything.

Serpio and *Argolito*

> Serpio—*According to Yaqui legend, a serpio is a giant
> animal that lives in canyons or caves, the most famous being
> a giant rattlesnake killed by an argolito at Cenyoa Boam in
> northern Mexico.*

> Argolito—*a little man from another world who streaks
> through the air with a long rope trailing behind him.*

The snake I killed was not the giant rattler
that lives in my spine.
The rattler I hacked to pieces was not
the *serpio* that aches in my spine.
The rope of the argolito hangs from
the cottonwood over the river,
sparks across the night sky as
the falling star of obedience.

The praying mantis that crawled up my leg
was not the *serpio* of the tangled vine.
The scorpion that bit me had a tail longer
than the rope of the *argolito*.
A giant pig chased me in a dream.
A man came out of nowhere to tell me his name.

I witnessed a battle between man and pig.
When the pig lay dying, I was promised the meat.
The food I consumed was fattened with guilt.
The source of the food sent me through the air.
The food I ate made me fat.
The source of food named me Gonzalez.
The *argolito* who whispered this to me
died the other day.
The *argolito* who left me didn't give me
time to learn his name.

II
The History of Desire

The History of Desire

based on ten photographs and paintings before the afterlife

Woman with Seven Iguanas on Her Head
photo by Graciela Iturbide

She is married to the Lizard Man, but left him
when the weight of the seven iguanas on her head
forced her to flee, to remove the tails as gifts of a marriage,
imprisonment that meant claws of the seven iguanas dug
into her neck each night, while her husband
and his lizards slept, her seven iguanas perched
on her head like a billowing hat, watching over her.

The woman with the seven iguanas stares ahead,
creatures finding room to sit on top of her,
a woman's hair long enough to hold
the clinging bodies as the seven reasons for love:

One for the black eyes of the iguana that witnesses each thought.

Two for the overhanging ability of the creatures to grasp what she sees.

Three for the cluster of scaled bodies that grant her permission to move.

Four for her head that knows the warmth of cold blood.

Five for the man whose hands tossed the iguanas onto her head.

Six for the love of the hiss, the claw, and the whip of the tail.

Seven for the woman who turns her head in all directions.

Her eyes are wide and black,
no smile, no jewelry around her neck.

The woman in the photo stands defiantly.
She has driven the world back.

The iguanas cling to her with jaws closed.
The iguanas hang like proud birds that despise wings.

Her eyes do not blink.
She will not allow the iguanas to fall from her head.

She leaves Oaxaca, heads north with the iguanas.
They cover her path, they read minds.

She leaves her husband without saying good-bye.
The shadows of iguana tails leave a message for him.

*

El Arte Ritual de la Muerte Niña (The Ritual Art of Child Death)
painting from the 19th century, artist unknown

Child Death is an expression that does not refer directly to the death of children, but rather to a Mexican cultural phenomenon, the ritual in which recently deceased children are no longer considered children but rather angelítos *(cherubs, or little angels), and as such their death is celebrated rather than mourned. It is not death per se; instead it is a joyful birth into another world.*
—historian José Gorostiza

The painting reads: El niño Miguel Reinoso se retrato a la edad de tres años y fallecio el día 8 de Junio a la auna de la mañana de 1816. *(Miguel Reinoso was painted at the age of three and died on the eighth of June at one in the morning in 1816.)*

Miguel holds a small tomato in his right hand.
He places it against his heart.
His left hand holds a white hat
that matches his pants and shirt.
A fine, black velvet coat prepares him for death.
He does not smile but knows the other world
waits for the tomato, his hat,

for the clean and short black hair
his mother combed before she knew
he was going to die.
Miguel believes in angels, but has never seen one.
He chose the tomato after dreaming
of row upon row of tomato plants
the day he was born.
He has no way of saying this.

He dies with the empty fields burned by his father,
watching from his mother's lap as the fires
line the earth with a path of escape.
Miguel dies at the age of three,
celebrated as the one who never spoke,
only gazed at the silence of the house,
the hot adobe walls, preparations for a harvest
he would never understand.
Miguel as the one who never spoke,
whose entry into the mountain is running red,
thick with the juice of his father's tomatoes,
crushed into his heart the morning of death.

*

Zapata at Nineteen
             oil on canvas by Alfredo Arreguin

The stolen face of the young hero
has nothing to do with the maze
of colors rising behind his profile.
Zapata at nineteen has nothing to do
with the revolution of the mind.

His Indian mother and father told him too much.
He hides behind the intricate triangles,
codices, and hieroglyphics of a language
he has no need to decipher.

His army waits for him.
His guns can be found behind the patterns
of blue, red, green, and orange blocks—
pyramid of destruction he will topple someday.

The brown face of Zapata has nothing to do
with the worship of his name.
It will not rise a century later when Chiapas
and its people suddenly appear in the painting.

They, too, are well hidden to the eye.
They are going to be glazed into
the hanging wall of words, cries,
groans, and vowels that spell

the color of rage, fine black wands
of Zapata's mustache pointing
to the first spot of color dabbed
onto the canvas by patient hands.

*

Baile con la Talaca (Dance with the Skeleton)
lithograph by Luis Jimenez

The *vato* is finally dancing.
      He is tall, proud, and muscular,
            his weary, hungover face managing a smile
for the skeleton   that moves with him.
She twirls her skirt,
      will take it off for him later,
spins now
      with her long, white hair
flowing   from her skull of love.
The *vato* has jumped awkwardly,
his brain   still frying   from the night before,
greasy hair stuck to his head,
      the T-shirt sweating a ring of gold
for the woman who wears no shirt,

the woman whose ribs gleam white
and straight   against his hardness.

The *vato* is finally dancing.
         He wraps his arms around her bony waist,
pulls her to him   and whispers,
"I love your coldness,
         your mouth,
the smell   of the worms   in your hair.
         Vamonos a mi casa."
The *vato* is the king of the streets.
         The next day he wakes in his bed.
and wonders what it was
         she said,
the howling   that made him come.
         He looks down where she lay,
but she is gone,
         leaving a dust,
brown and white grains of soil
         floating,
still excited in the air.

*

This Mother Ain't for Sale
         stoneware sculpture by Marsha Gomez

Stoneware sculpture of a crucified woman goddess
reminds me how once I saw her up in the tree,
huge stone breasts covered by clay bowls

that held the tip of the sun on them,
light burning through the nipples I wanted to touch,
so I could believe I was going to be loved, someday.

Her arms are cut off at the elbow,
spread out like the arms of Jesus
who beat her to the cross.

She wears a white necklace that sweats
between the breasts I touched as a boy,
her crown of Mayan mirrors resembling

the image opening my eyes when
I first buried my face in her breasts.
She closes her eyes to me,

wide lips opening the air of learning,
spell of a small boy wondering why
he couldn't have her in the still frame,

in the smell of dirt, the molding of her face
and chest appearing to him when he walked alone
in search of her missing arms.

*

My Body Standeth over Still
acrylic by Timoteo Ikoshy Montoya

The man with the horns stands on the water
        of the purple lake, his black tree of desire
rising up from the water.
        His red skirt is dry,
never gets wet when he comes across the lake
        to steal someone back.
He wears a lone feather around his neck,
        his naked chest smooth and clean
as if he wanted another man to touch him.
        The man with the horns knows something.
It is why he smirks into the sun,
        looks across the water as he stands still
for those who want him,
        those who believe the position of sex
and power lies under the water
        where he tossed a mutilated turtle,
bit off its head to gain his horns,
        making sure his tree would grow.

The man with the horns keeps them clean.
    Their white-and-black tips have burned before.
He pulled them out before she screamed.
    He is not going to tell.
He doesn't know.
    He won't admit the purple-and-pink water
at his feet has something to do with the way
    he betrayed his faith,
black hills behind him enclosing the final chance
    for the bodies he wanted to swim
to him and take him by his dripping legs.

*

La Casa de la Bestia (**The Beast's House**)
    mixed media on paper by Javier Arevalo

Twisted horses
                Flying horses
            Broken horses
Bent
horses
        Because the house of the beast
belongs to the horse that gave me a wish,
allowed me to ride it

years after my grandfather fell off,
        his head hitting the rock
as if the walls of the beast
        were going to open for him.

Horseshoes everywhere

Trails of horseshoes

Alphabet formed by horseshoes

The path of my grandfather's broken head

The horseshoe as the luck of the dead

The horseshoe as the glowing brand of history

where any ancestor I never met sings about me
in a song composed to surround the horses,
drive them into the corral where they count them,
mistake them, hound them, punish them,
       make them angry,
torture them,
        get them ready for the ride
of the victorious thieves
who believed the house of the beast
       was the home of the invincible traveler.

Three green horseshoes
Three upside-down adobe arches

Too many mud walls keeping the horse
inside the house of the beast

The door of his mane
The hoof of his heart

The sound of his snorting
The mistake of his legs

Clustered walls showing me
how the horse is the symbol
I can't understand

because the family tale about
the three horses that got away
bothers me with the fact

each animal wore
green horseshoes scorched that color
by the mad blacksmith

who told the family
three lost sons had far to go
before they could dismount

count their losses
forget how many miles it was
from their pounding hearts

to the hooves that broke
followed them
to their brown-and-black deaths

*

Five Yaqui Masks *(Arizona State Museum)*

At last, I see where my grandmother came from.
She has worn the five masks.
I have seen them on her ninety-three-year-old face.

I saw the first one as a one-year-old.
It was the mask of nutrition.
The green face of love.
The red cheeks of care.
The white eyes of the storyteller
who lifted me in one hand, flew me
in the air above her as votive candles
in the room changed the colors of her mask.

The second mask is the tongue of the cook.
The blue face of the silent burn.
The yellow eyes who have seen too much death.
The blue nose of the one who creates
a soup of onions, cactus greens, chiles, potatoes,
secret leaves the color of goat blood,
and the skin of the pig, guts of the cow
that always has its own mask.

The third is the mask of anger.
The way she hit my alcoholic uncle
with the flyswatter, whacked him many times
as he shouted and cried in the kitchen,
the drunk coming home at four in the morning
to make her put on her brown-and-orange mask,
the green eyes blending the cry of tequila
with the shards of beer-bottle glass that exploded,
didn't penetrate the mask of a boiling cloud
that took over the house to make sure
the son had no mask.

The fourth is the look of the midget.
The profile of the secret keeper.
The long strands of the white-haired woman
who is shrinking, paying off her debts,
folding into herself to keep from having to wear
another brown mask full of hair,
her eyes and mouth growing under
the world of the punished hair.

The last one is a death mask.
The tiny black eyes of knowledge.
Red cheeks and nose of the mother.
Triangular yellow mask of the one who loved
a whole century without giving up her country,
without going back to the mountains of the Yaqui dead
who gave her these faces for love, for hate,
faces of the year she fell back into the mountains
to create the mask not yet named.

*

Ex-Voto

oil on canvas by Nahum B. Zenil

Hand with a knife
        piercing the heart.
The massive heart

             hanging in the air,
thick arteries like tentacles
       of the man who shields
himself from the weaker heart.
         The hand penetrates
the chambers.
        The other man stands
behind the heart.
         His shirt is open.
He has short hair of the prisoner.
          Above them
is the painting of La Virgen de Guadalupe,
       the only one whose heart
will never be exposed.
        She watches over everything,
allows the knife and the prisoner,
         his killer hand to live,
so she can offer a second chance,
       further punishment
for the way they lived,
         second drama
in the bloody story of how those
       who believe in her
are going to pay.

*

Burning Dreams

    oil on canvas by Carlos Almaraz

At last, my neighborhood is burning down.
The houses have missiled into flames.

No one can stop the fire.
No one will rebuild.

At last, the house of desire where I was born
is going up in smoke.

The Path of the Dragons

In ancient China, the Lung Meis were lines
on hilltops connecting to each other.

Atop each hill, the dragons kept their nests,
flew over the lines, from nest to nest,

their aerial paths tracing the lines without wandering
off to chase lightning bolts that pounded the hills

closer and closer to the nests,
searching for signs of birth.

The dragons never failed to feed their babies
right before they were blinded by the new sun.

The older dragons knew when to drop the humans
into the open mouths of their young,

filling them with the answer to the tale,
changing the way the lines marked the earth,

sacrificing their nourished litter to the lightning
created by the collector of wings

as they were electrocuted into eternity,
burned into myth.

The Hawk in the Yard

It stands in the grass the morning before Christmas,
its prey torn apart in its claws,
feathers scattered over the yard, piercing
yellow eyes staring straight ahead, in between
pecks at red meat that glistens in the sun.
Its white chest is streaked with brown markings,
a hawk in our yard surprising us by coming close,
eating as if something will be taken.
The hawk looks about and clutches the meat,
turns in the early light so I can see it,
not knowing I watch as it pulls a string
of intestine out of its catch,
tosses the tiny heart onto the grass,
these things sharp through my binoculars,
eyes of the hawk staring at what I can't
describe as it pecks and tears.

I look through the glasses, see a hawk surviving
in the frozen yard of a dying year, predator
taking a chance by landing in the yard,
weight of its prey forcing it here to eat.
The morning sun slashes across its wings
to show me there is no time for surprise.
Nothing will move or die without the hawk.
Nothing will be torn without reason,
no second chance to learn how a meal
is the defiant act of winter—the last ripping
of fear the hawk may be a wrong sign.
This hawk precedes the harvest, but its pull
at the meat is a gift for the new year,
stark abundance dripping as the hawk
takes it in its claws and flies.

The Turtle

I found a dead turtle in the dirt lot
    across from my house.
Its head had been cut off, stiff claws
    and wrinkled legs sticking out
of its shell like a tiny man who let
    the world fall on him.
Someone crushed the turtle into the sand
    like the tribe forcing the prisoner
to kneel in the red soil where
    they abolished his beliefs.
Someone crushed the turtle, left it
    in the weeds as the shiny coin
that marks the path.

I stood over it in fear,
    a twelve-year-old who had not seen
opened life before, knew the shell
    gave strength to those who wanted
to climb inside a shattered bowl
    of ugly wisdom.
I stared at the remains of the turtle,
    saw its geometric shape grow into
the soil as if dried blood formed a sign
    it was going to rise and hiss at me.

I stepped back, smelled an odor I didn't know,
    thought I saw movement.
Staring at the turtle drew me into an old dream
    where I ran after a pack of dogs
who galloped ahead of me, trying
    to keep up with an enormous black shape
they chased into the canyons.
    I ran after the dogs, their barks
disappearing when they were swallowed
    by what they chased, the thing

that entered the canyons becoming
    the turtle lying down,
too slow to know, too old to live within
    its head that expands and contracts
for birth, the impact that sends us both
    to the ground, weight of what caught us
with a hush of beauty and forgiveness.

Two Striped Lizards

They look like miniature orange-and-brown tigers
clinging to the concrete blocks in the backyard,

two lizards looking up at me as I lift the wood
off their hiding place.

They stick to the bricks, flatten themselves except
for their heads and enlarged eyes, tiny faces

looking curious and human, staring at me
when I move, blinking as if I were going to grab them,

one of them springing out of the brick, disappearing
into the grass to lead me away from their home.

Two striped lizards are a good omen for the man
who knew the reptiles that led him to the well.

Two striped lizards are signs of abundant thirst,
plenty of water, their rapid movement and caution

leaving me with something to grasp—a blade of grass,
an abandoned spider web, a concrete block I won't move

because I learned what the striped lizard means—
a tiger in the canyon is as good

as the escaped dragon of the heart—
the second lizard not moving

as I leave it alone and close the lid
on the muffled source of its trembling.

San Antonio Marauder

The lost journeys make no sense.
When I return, there is music in the air.
The bloody Christ on the wall is smiling.
Black dogs in the backyards are growling.
The lost journeys make no sense.
A dozen beer bottles lined up on the back fence.
When I hide in another house on Guadalupe Street,
no one notices, no one cares.

The hands of the workers in the tortilla factory
slap hot plates all day.
My god slaps my face all day.
I hide in the tiny room and smell the cockroaches.
Some of them fly into my hair.
The lost journey will have to make sense.
I hear an old piano playing somewhere.
It is the homeboy next door tapping his knives
against the back of his younger brother,
telling him to lie down and be still.
When the young boy hides his face in the pillow
and cries, the police car slowly goes by.

The bloody Christ on the wall is folding his hands,
torn palms springing away from the cross,
his face staring at me as if this is the last house.
When I hide in a new home,
a woman will be waiting for me.
I have known her name for many years.
My poems belong to her
and the lost cats in the house.
When I enter her room for the first time,
she whispers something about snow clouds.
When I sit in the chair, she rubs my head as I cry.
There is no one outside.
If there was, I would not ask for her breasts,

her way of rubbing her fingers into
the wounds on the soles of my feet,
cutting my will to run from the step
I took before I learned to live.

*

My heart stopped when I loved.
My stomach reflected passages when I wrote
how rosaries become pillows fastened to a thief.
I owned rusted cans in the kitchen that fed eighteen bald men,
found graffiti on doors, wrote a book to erase those thoughts.
When I waited for someone to arrive, I opened my book of flowers,
my book of wires, my book of directions to follow pages.

I slept between the sound of gunfire and drive-bys,
screeching tires of patrol cars branding the night with
tenement frames that burned down with my need.
I saw trash-can flies buzz over the head of an old drunk
who pointed a bloody finger at me.
I saw the brown body of the stripper dancing in the street,
cabaret lights singing with the smell of sperm, wasted men
cursing her in Spanish without a name for their beers.

*

Fire ants grow over the hills and valleys.
They stream from the shallow creeks,
mistake me for nourishment.
When I hide in the arch of a tree, I wear no mask,
drink the tequila of death, and recite two or three ways.
They pray for me in the stalls,
step out of the way when the tornado arrives.
They think I will be here to warn them not to lie.

When I leave the cracking doors of the church,
I see no saints, no absolution in the stones
falling from the well into the hole of the devil.
When I leave the pale walls of the woman's house,

I see no books, only a commitment to stay
and be told this is where the breast meets the prayer.
I lift an old wooden slab from the tall grass
in our newly bought yard.
Seven or eight black widows spring out
and run for my feet.

There

There is the voice of confinement in the pinecone,
a prism of laughter hiding in one shoulder,
mistaking the naked back for the need to run.
There is the chamber of how you fall into the hunt,
speaking so fast, you become the green chameleon
hiding on the back porch of the house,
swelling his throat into the crimson bubble
that belongs to the eclipse.

There is the ritual of the mud and onion that won't grow,
a hummingbird becoming text, beating the bee to the pollen
that wasted years getting to the numbing spore, caught
in your throat when you found no water came from your sweat,
the error of holding down the temperature of the earth.
There is the shape of the stomach and the wasp drawn
upon the neck, a red scratch from white and pink roses growing
west, fungus on their brown leaves you carried in your mind.

There is the manner of becoming two men,
one for the asking and one for holding onto the son
who abandoned your home to dance with his real father,
commissioned by boys to run wild in the streets,
leaving you to wonder which words you overlooked
in the graffiti that took days to wash over.
There is the fire large enough to hold the toys you miss—
a box of dry weeds, an empty carton of milk,
a small wooden ball so light, you toss it in the air
and call your third-grade friends to come back.

There is the beetle glistening in the pueblo, spelling
"no" with its black wings, green and silver bands crawling
up your arm the night you lay in the dirt, had to tell a lie
in order for those boys to let you up. You told them how
you grew two heads on your shoulders—one for love,
one for fleeing before the flooded river,

the course every swarming beetle takes.
These sounds were tied to your ears by string
you cut off a kite, wound around one leg of the *chicharra*
that swallowed you as you rose from your rocking chair,
an old man eating the wings of flying things
landing in the bowl set before his broken legs.

The Finger Moth

The finger moth alights in the shadows
of what has been—brushes my knuckles
with the right to be defeated by
the kissing beauty of my hands.
The finger moth folds into the century
where love will be a mountainside,
the fluttering inside my farthest reach.

The finger moth dissolves into
the verdict of my eyelashes,
moves in and out of the shadows,
lands on the chair where my father
wished for nothing, sat in his T-shirt
and drove himself out of the light.

The finger moth is petrified
in the bathroom mirror, but
where are the men to show me
mirrors always sit in front
of the faces of shaving men?

The finger moth cuts itself
into the glass, tattoos its shape
into the lines and codes of wings.
When I turn to leave the room,
it is night and the moth answers.
I can't leave, can't see there
is something for me to breathe.

The finger moth explodes into
a clattering of threads, blinding
prisms there and not there.
I can't leave, until the finger moth
is gone like the chair my father carved

out of his past, its wooden legs trembling
beyond my face in the mirror,

the room welcoming the shadows
with nothing expected, no light
washing my clean hands
as they reach for the moth.

From the Face

Each night the Gila monster enters
the house of the daughter,
lies down in the exception of water,
and disappears for forty-five years.

Each morning the hanged man comes
down off the tree and enters the town,
each whisper memorized, his footsteps
sounding like his children forgive him
and finally call him "Father."

Each evening the blind crosses are torn off
the church walls, piled in a tower
that never falls, until the tired ones
stop breathing and ignite the flames.

Each night the horizon praises its own beauty
and disappears, arrives at dawn before
the stricken country recognizes the threat
of mountains lying between one storm
and the one morning flower.

⌣

IV
The Poor Angel

Esé

Esé, I saw you scream
in the brown waters of the barrio,
found you sleeping in the fist
of the polluted moon,
a broken beer bottle
in your heaving chest.
You were my friend
in the story of the tortillas
that fed us, made us fatter
as the border changed course
with the restless river.

I saw you boil the soup
to extract a daze
out of your dagger,
dim fires that masqueraded
as warmth from your cut-off hands,
stumps flying in the blood
of the gang that celebrated you.
You wanted to cross the wire
one more time, mud charted
to flow south toward
your killing dream.

You lifted the mountains
to touch your sweating chest,
carried something in your pockets
of rags and ripped desire.
You were hung on the wall
as a brown shadow
I gave up long ago.

We were in the dirt streets
that flooded when it rained.
We ran ahead of the rising water,

crossed the corners as cars splashed us,
made us dodge flying mud
as it formed into faces lying
down in the sinking streets.

The Poor Angel

One morning I notice someone passes by.
She looks like the poor woman from across the street,
her family destroyed in the earthquake.
  Her house is nothing but adobe dust,
    straw, and wooden beams broken into the first forms
    of the cross I recognized outside of any church.

Beside the beggar's knife,
I will rejoin the dove.
Beside the wine that is the blood of the gang leader,
    I will fill the bottle with quarters.
    Beside the car painted with graffiti,
    a street sign that says, "One Way."

                              *

Tacho prays a lie.
He believes in the devil.
The tattoo on his arm proves it.
Tacho prays a lie.
He wears a hat and sunglasses.
He used to be in the navy, was my father
before I was born.
He used to love my mother before divorce.
Tacho prays a lie.
He cut himself with a razor trying to erase
the horns and tail from his skin.

                              *

      Asking for the pomegranate to dissolve in my mouth,
I spit two or three seeds, red juice marking me
as the one who told the truth, decapitated fruit redder
in my open palm, seeds rolling out, some of them falling
to the floor for me to step on, crush them into red stars

flying farther than Tacho's angel.

   Taking the pomegranate means there is a bare tree
that lied to me, made up a story about a man and wife
remaining perfect, seeds of the pomegranate hiding
on their tongues to be taken out by soft hands.

   Sucking on the tiny seeds means there is a nub,
a nipple, a promise to grow old beyond the tree
that escaped the year of the moss, time of the fungus,
season of the purple streak that crossed the earth,
changed the fruit into the sweetest lie enjoyed by men.
They pick the pomegranate at the right weight,
correct hardness, the red globe they hang between their legs,
transformed into the scrotum waiting to be plucked
by the lover's hand.

*

Tacho on fire.
Tacho hosting the party.
Tacho and his sandals.
Tacho and his mustache.
Tacho and the hidden bag of Sensimilla buds.
Tacho and the cross on the wall.

Tacho and the glowing cross on the wall at night.
Tacho in his bed looking up in the dark at the glowing Christ.
Suddenly, something gets in the way.
Something blocks the glow.
Tacho on fire.
Tacho hosting the party.

*

I came from El Paso, from the border of angry bees
and brown dogs who stick their torn snouts into the river.
I came from the border of twisted wire
and the pregnant woman floating in the water.

I came from the mountain with the cross carved on top,
the boundaries where the insides of doors are painted
the colors of superstition—swirls of lavender, pink,
and green blood to keep bad spirits away.

I came from the town of bad spirits that have no answer
to the brown petals of mud flowers covering
everything that moves, that wants to sing, that tastes
like the earth kissed the umbilical cord of every Mexican
man, woman, and child, then spit them out in disgust.

I came from the border where the cottonwoods
are misunderstood as petrified bodies of those who died
to be able to live in peace and drink the water
from contaminated canals of home.

I came from the last sound of women collecting prayers
in black shawls made from the hair of men who abandoned them.
I came from the line that surrounds every man
who tries to cross.
I came from El Paso that lies on this side.

*

A man was given one chance.
He turned it into a kiss that outburned
        the blade on his car hood.
He turned his chance into escape,
followed his shoes beyond the city lights.
        He saw the river and knew it was true.
The radiance of tomorrow was radioactive on his shoes.

A man was given one chance to build a house
out of a dead horse lying in the field,
        a farm out of soil that wouldn't turn black,
change his house into an old dream where his son comes back,
an ex-con hiding from the latest crime, the bodybuilder
        grunting in the backyard, dropping his weights
when the rattlesnake struck his leg from behind,

dropping the dumbbell to flatten the thing
that made his father come running for the first time.

*

The poor angel's name is Antonio.
He hovers over the poor and the forgotten dogs.
He plays timbales in the ghost band, eats thunder
and lightning and the rotten shells of discarded eggs.
The poor angel has been driven from heaven,
has often invaded hell.
Antonio wanders over the cemetery in the barrio.
He knows where everyone sleeps, why the young boy
standing before the gravestone of his great-grandmother
knows there is a secret buried there, something
the poor angel wants to share.
It rains when the boy brings flowers in rusted cans.
The cemetery floods in the storm, makes the boy
find shelter by the great stone gates.

It was the angel who opened the tomb, a black cloud
that gave the boy the urge to find objects in the grave,
things his great-grandmother left him at age five—
a bright red rosary, the crucifix of mahogany
brought from San Luis Potosí, the faded drawing
of a man standing by a church, the sketch of a woman
with long hair sending an odor across the cemetery grounds.

The poor angel wants to tell the boy what it means,
why the tiny box of tin the boy can't open is the find,
the thing it traps inside made for only one man,
the fingerbone clattering inside the box as the boy
gathers the objects, looks to the sky and runs
when he sees there are poor angels coming out of the ground,
wanting to guide him, poor angels without hands
trying to surround him as he runs.

*

Tacho comes back.
He hid in an old '56 Chevy his father left in the dirt lot.
Tacho tries to sleep it off, but hears a noise in the night.
He rises from the torn backseat, looks through the broken window
to find the black pig has returned.

The animal stands looking up at him, its fat, greasy skin
shining in the night, its low grunts telling him
the sign of the black pig was good and bad luck,
time to finally jump out of the car and go inside the house,
beg his father for a place to sleep.

*

There was the touch of ash on my forehead.
　　　　I closed my eyes.
The smell of incense carried me to a stone wall
　　　　where two naked old men heaved rocks onto their shoulders.
There was the touch of holy water over my eyes.
　　　　The smell of the church scared me.
Fainting, I was led out by my angry mother.
　　　　She scolded me, told me God had a face
and was going to punish me.

There was the touch of someone passing behind me
　　　　to kneel at the first pew.
I turned to look into the crowd of worshipers,
　　　　but didn't know who it was.
There was the smell of death, an oath to life,
　　　　chanting that hit me across the face
as my mother and I fell out into the blinding sunlight
　　　　on the other side of the heavy sanctuary doors.

*

I'm more than the man who gives up
and says, "I was the one who ran away,
the holder of the candle and maker of the clay."

I'm more than the whisper the family finds
when they sit down to eat.
They recognize me in time to scold me,

tell me I can't be told anything because
my eyes were blinded by a wild tale of
some poor angel hitting me on the head.

I'm more than the man who gives up,
who wants to wear a bead around his neck
that means nothing more than I found it

shining on my walk across the hills,
the blue-and-orange glass hovering over
the thorns, waiting for me to pick it up.

I don't want to be told that wearing it
is a sign of belief in something else,
a mirror of the angel who waits for me.

I'm more than the man who dreams of a claw
holding him down,
not letting him breathe,

who believes in the heat of arrivals when
the Savior comes down to cut the claw
and let him go.

I'm more than the man who left the desert,
who fingers the rosary while hiding
in the cottonfields of the Rio Grande.

I'm more than the one who knows
what is hidden in the ruins,
who can read the graffiti on cracked walls,

more than the person who saw the wings
scattering the seed across the river to sow
one or two floods so nothing grows.

I'm more than the one who let Tacho go
without a hug, who created his father
to show any boy what it is.

I'm more than you, whose future
is sequined with permission, until there
is nothing left for those who survive with

strong women who hate you if you say no,
if you tell the truth and pray to a wrong god,
tell them they must create a family with men

who are more than men, the ones who don't
need a tree, or a long piece of wood, one or two
timbers, hammers and nails, a sacrifice—

they don't need the great arch to survive
and still be willing to be mounted
on the bloody cross.

Without Villages

The June heat exiles our needs.
Streets melt in hundred and ten degree heat.
The enormous pot of *menudo* boils on the stove.
In the Lopez bakery, *bonillos* are nineteen cents.
Four cinnamon cookies for thirty cents.
The baker comes out drenched in sweat.

Someone is going to collect a knife today.
The motorcycle cop knocks on the wrong door.
The homeless vato drops dead, only
to wake up as a fox terrier in another life.
No one knows about this.
My uncle told me about him.
He didn't know his name.
He loved the dog.
It got hit by a car.
The vato never came back after that.

Even here, in another room,
the brain hums in the night.
It is like a pickled pig's foot embracing
the old *cuento* of the fat Mocoso breaking
into the restaurant at night,
shattering all the dishes as he ate
the leftover *chicharrónes, tripas,*
the cold rice pounded into trash bags
to be set out in the morning.
Mocoso even ate two huge bags of tostadas.
The police never found him.
They ate in the restaurant one morning
and knew why he broke in.

*

Let's repeat the song of the center
where the beautiful girl decides
she is going to save the world
by taking off her clothes for a dirty, old guy
who is a friend of her father's.
They do it at his house and she is surprised
at how much she liked it.

Her father finds out.
He shoots the guy.
She is not surprised her father does six years.
By the time he gets out, she is a single mother
with three kids, on welfare, a bruised cheek,
and has not seen their father in several months.

She is beautiful after all this because the song
has something to do with the father who did time
and the mother who kept silent for years,
helpless to do anything about her daughter.

*

Unknown fountains.
The drum wrapped around the head of a fish.

Coughing tigers lying down to die.
The priest begging the Lord not to teach him more prayers.

Smashed acoustic guitars mounted inside a volcano.
Early tickets to the bus ride.

Late moves down the mountain where a tribe vanished
never to be discovered or dug up.

The hero waiting for the bus from Chihuahua to arrive.
Unnamed sources of disease eating the human body.

Four billion cells cavorting on the tip of the nose.
The watercolor artist dipping her brushes in milk.

Running doves landing in water.
An odd three-inch orange-and-green bug

with transparent wings that look like combs
brushing the hair of a happy woman.

An attempt to skip each and every vowel
and get to the message in the glass of water.

A tired man organizing a festival.
Electric wires in a heart of an ape who knows there is a God.

Fears that the truth contains the whole story.
Courage to dismantle the bread rolls and pass them

among the rich, the wealthy, the ones who
would devour them without saying a word.

Marriage as the giving and guessing of what
the other desires when there is time to believe

every breath we lock away for each other
is every year we outlive those who don't care.

Invocations and the redeemers gunned down.
A fat city full of crime, fires, smoke,

broken glass, mistaken identities,
neon signs, paved roads.

A fresh bowl of hot, green chile sauce branding
the lips of a sweating boy who went into the place

because someone was following him,
someone wanted to teach him about the seeds.

The Angels of Juárez, Mexico

Sometimes, they save people from drowning in the river.
Their faces are the color of the water,
wings soaked in the oil of crossing
keeping them from leaving the border.
The oldest angel is a man from the last century
whose white hair hangs to the ground.
He floats above the water each time he saves
a *mojado* who tries to cross in the raft,
falling into the current to be somebody.

The angels of Juárez look over the *colonias,*
nibble on the cardboard shacks like the rats
they never fear because rats have their own angels.
When children fall into the poison waters,
the angels dance above the glowing waves,
pull out the chosen child with a kiss,
toss him on the bank for others to find.

These angels know about revolution and dying,
prefer to hover over the Rio Grande,
where the bodies move at night,
fighting for air some angels mistake
as a grasp toward heaven.

The angels of Juárez sometimes hide
from the desire to cross,
to take a chance and send a chant
over the dirty waters, the latest
drowning victim wondering
why the tired old man he was told
to look for never extended a hand.

The angels appear in the night,
listen to the crush of water as the course
of the border tightens with searchlights

and the hidden green cars of patrol.
They swim over the electricity,
wings humming to create a magnet
that makes it easier to cross.

The angels don't know
something is going to end.
They don't appear near the churches,
the missions, or the kneeling altars.
They are not part of the prayer,
the ritual, or the escape.
They know the river is moving faster,
churning toward the horizon
that accepts fewer souls each year.

The angels hover to make sure
the water keeps flowing,
mud of the barefoot moving
to the other side of the river where
no angels dwell because this side
was cleared of faith long ago,
waiting streets of El Paso never
mistaken for the place of angels.

White

Written after several treks through White Sands National Monument, New Mexico, site of Trinity, the first atomic bomb explosion, 1945. My parents were in high school at the time and told me El Pasoans, that day, saw a white flash in the sky one hundred miles to the north.

The White Silence

The white silence is absolved.
It murmurs in the body and heaves.
It sees me and arms itself with warmth.
The white silence is a reward
worth the wet hair and angry eye.
It shifts into a love for tears and windows.
The white silence is feeding,
it thinks of me coming back talking,
but to talk would be a white noise from
white flowers I stepped on long ago.

The White Iguana

The white iguana sits on my wife's head.
Its tail covers her eyes.
She can't know I am coming back.
The white iguana prays on the head
of the woman I have loved for years.
When I open my eyes, the iguana hisses,
combs the hair of my wife with its claws.
When my wife opens her eyes,
the white iguana loves the light,
leaps off her head and flies.

The White Tarantula

The white tarantula crawled out of my heart,
moved down my chest and brushed my nipples.
The white iguana visited me in my sleep.
When I woke, it waited, hidden somewhere in the room.
When I woke, I had crossed to the other side,
was no longer afraid.
The white tarantula denies it came out of my heart.
When I search for it in my room,
its absence tells me it is back in my blood.

The White Tree

The white tree grew at my window.
One night, I heard someone climb its branches.
When I went to look, a white shadow crossed
itself, then disappeared.
In two days, the white tree died.
The first night of its decay, I could not sleep.
The white tree shed its light.
When I sat up in bed, its leaves were singing
and changing color in the air.

The White Hair

I found the white hair sticking to my shirt.
When I plucked it between two fingers,
I saw it was the hair that grew on my head.
I found the white hair was twisted, tiny knots
bending its fiber like a line on a map.
I found the white hair and thought she was gone.
When I looked in the mirror, my entire head was white.
I dropped the white hair in surprise.
It disappeared as it hit the floor.
When I looked in the mirror, my entire head was black.

The White Guitar

The white guitar was stolen from my closet.
When I found it was gone, music came through the walls.
I went into the other room, but no one was there.
The white guitar had twelve strings,
given to me by my father before he died.
I played it only once, the day before I left.
I thought I could touch what had already been sung,
but I hid the guitar in the closet for years.
Then, it was stolen from my home.
When I open my doors, I still hear the strumming
and there is a song.

The White Fountain

The white fountain sprays a mist over the streets,
shoots higher, and all is cold.
The white fountain collects coins and wets the dog,
soaks me when I walk.
The white fountain blinds me when I pause,
water rising from the thirst for love.
The white fountain is a cloud that cleans me,
freezes in midair when I have a name.

The White Room

I found it in my forty-sixth year.
The white room opened and shared its furniture.
When I entered, I found a huge bed
the size of desire.
The white room was empty, but kept me.
When I sat in the white chair, I thought of plants.
When I lay on the cold bed, I had no words.
The white room kept me forty-six years.
When I rose to leave, I had no ideas.
When I touched the doorknob, all the windows opened.

The White Sirens

The white sirens called when the city burned.
They shattered my ears and gave me hope.
I walked the streets and saw black buildings.
The white sirens shrieked with hope.
I hid in the alleys and waited for smoke.
The white sirens showed me the way.
When they rose in a deafening sword,
I found the shoe in the trash can.
The white sirens drove me out of town.
When I listened, all I heard was the wailing,
the cry to look up at the oncoming sky.

The White Cars

The white cars followed me into September.
They were everywhere like crickets.
When I hid in the barrio, headlights danced.
When I crossed the street, I was the traffic.
The white cars were full of gasoline.
They waited at intersections, engines thriving.
When I thought of waving one down, I cried.
The white cars followed me into the world.
When I recognized one driver, he was my father,
age twenty, returning from the U.S. Navy.

The White Streets

The white streets have no home.
I walk them in search of fame,
find nothing but white dirt in my socks.
Signs on street corners spell "God" in Spanish.
The white streets have no lanes,
lead to the desert,
but the desert is no longer there.
I watch boys fight on asphalt and let them gain.

I cross and cross and never get lost.
The white streets have no seasons.
I return from white dunes and am touched.
I return on them and no one knows,
come back to be greeted by a glowing, white cross.

Lifted White

They told me to lift my head and watch
the sun kiss the radiating century good-bye.
I lifted my soul instead and was blinded
by the flash my spirit released.
They told me to let go of my past
so I could see how many miracles
I could find in the fever of loneliness.
I gave them our history instead,
was blessed with knowing how many years
it would take to say, "I am no longer afraid."

They told me to embrace the child
on either side of my path, listen
to their weeping as if it were my own.
I told them to sing, instead,
gave them years to end their songs.
When they let go of my hands,
I was too old to understand.

Thinking the century was over,
I lay down to die.
When I opened my eyes,
I was still there and saw
the white light was one god,
with one hand, pulsing its defiant veins.

V
Sentora

Brown Pot

And so I eat from a brown pot,
sticking my fingers into
the stomach of the seed,
smearing them with laughter
and the growling voice.
I eat the brown eye, its carving
pupil leaving my sight
to enter ladders of fingers—
mistaken bellies of hungry fools.
And so I eat from a brown hand,
opening the leaves to fill the room—
odors, smells, gases from the juice
my father extracted when he fried
a goat and called it God.

I eat from a brown pot,
greasy sides glistening with words
I first learned when I was full—
like anguish, hope, stand up.
Spit the stem from the woven heart.
I swallow the chasing worm,
mutation of protein and tired tooth,
making me taste digested truth
that escapes the wind no man calls
his own without a name.
And so I sit and belch and need,
wishing the picked bone was used
to trace lines on my face,
the way the cook cut her hands
and fed the pot to make it brown.

I eat from a forgotten brain—
scooping thoughts out of the skull,
licking the bone to see again as I
listen for the hum of the tongued ear.

I eat from the first body, asking
for crumbs to come alive,
change hunger into the shape
of smoked-out rooms where women
chanted, cooked fear into a *masa*
to shape the man, take him
into the world for years to come.
And so I eat from a brown pot
on the greasy table, fill myself
with chewing voices, shards
of clay sticking in my throat,
the deepest swallowing before
stuffing myself with the livers
of what is fed to me.

Sentora

*Sentora—the being who dwells inside abandoned adobe
huts. Sentoras are only attracted to shelters of mud.*

It hangs from a dry well, vibrates with
the footsteps of the drowned man who came back
to find the only Sentora this side of the Rio Grande.

It crawls up the well to take over the house of the man
who returned, its spreading patterns of holy skin becoming
the final snake he killed with his bare hands, ripping the head

off to tempt Sentora to come out of the water.
Sentora belongs to the moving ground of what he owns
and what he possesses, the shape of its moist crown inhabiting

the thoughts of those who lie in the reopened house.
Sentora shines in green and lost crimson, its flowering shield
leaving pieces of bread on the floors of bare rooms.

The man wakes from a cold cry, a calling he heard when
his father told him Sentora would return to change the sky.
He sees there are signs of Sentora in the room,

how it watched him as he slept. The walls breathe yellow,
the windows shot with webs of confession, one or two
twigs of prayer lying on the dirt floor.

The bread has changed into wafers of communion he picks up,
clean and dirty, swallows them before Sentora returns.
He has seconds to tell the truth to himself, leave out

the lie of his life because it belongs to Sentora—
its love for the brown men of the hot dirt.
In his final step behind the shattered door,

he sees how he treated his family,
how they let him go as he worshiped the thorn
and the white rock, told them the arroyo in the rain

is the direction he would take.
Sentora pushes the door with a whisper
and takes the drowned man.

The Cult of the Closed Hand

Begins with the fingernail smashed in an accident,
unsuccessful attempt at defending strength
hidden in each closed hand.

The tightened fist governs the color
of the fingernail secluded from companions
and the things they grip.

When the group joins hands, it hurts.
When they lavish touch upon their palms,
they give each other longer life lines in sweaty palms.

The cult of the closed hand was begun
when I had to find a way of touching someone
who knew the secret of the knuckles.

When the one I loved held my hand,
I knew the circle of her giving had never been disturbed.
I promised a fist for the raining vowels,

the cracking of bone that flies at us
without warning, as if the breaking of possessions
spells an end to the wrist.

Our closed hands remain inside the onion of the arm,
the strong scent of the star we carry in our armpit,
the farthest point of hiding fists.

I consider opening my hand to show you
how things a hand witnesses accumulate a weight
that reaches the hidden veins of the palm.

The cult of the closed sorrow is the enlarged finger
that points and traces the shape of our disfigurement,
sore muscular practice of welcoming you with open hands.

Still Life with Endings

For the cracked dish with
the dragon branded on it.
For the glazed finger in a sculpture
of a winged woman slipping
her mouth around the cock
of a man who has never known
the power of stone.
For the man who gives her his life
as rectangular landscape.
For the wheel of the mountain
ending in an earthquake no one felt.

For the mango sucked before
having to confess how many shadows
landed on the island.
For the voice interpreting a language
to children wanting to write
their first poems.
For husband and wife staying together
through the pain and joy of distance,
love growing with the vegetables
in the deep green shrubbery.

For the music written when
there was one child to sing it.
For the artist who left this mark
that will never be deciphered.
For the fish hiding under lily ponds
until darkness brings them out
in time for the diving osprey.
For pebbled ceilings following
the closeness of a family
who built the house, only to leave
when there was misunderstanding.
For high windows that reflect rain
that has no reason to fall.

For Mexican riddles and ghosts
from the sanctuary, rising
to change the direction
of the boy fleeing his country.
For an act of contrition
and the way forgiveness lies
without shadow in corners
of every possible image.
For the last elegy of a mother
wanting to be burned
so her children can forgive her.
For men visiting their dead fathers
in kitchens of strangers' houses.

For collecting dried pine needles,
trying to glue a design out of them
onto a piece of red wood.
For waiting to be given another
time and place, a uniform
of colored maples that sway
in a wind too strong for cottonwoods.
For the hope of asking a loved one
to select a mask from the closet.
For the crime of having too many
shirts that don't fit.
For the selection of souls
thrashing outside the door.
For the last meeting with a mentor
when no questions were asked.

For the time I was helpless
and had to take my vision down,
close my eyes and pretend
I was someone who did not
worry about losing my hands
in the stream of water pouring
out of the cliff when I reached it
after climbing for two days,
discovering this was the place

where I was tied down by invaders,
strapped to this table of rock,
pierced by holy vowels
that cut into my wrists.

Beyond Having

And, always, there is desire like
the orange and banana changing
texture on the kitchen shelf.
Their skins sink slowly into themselves.
There is the liquid of lust and thirst,
an open gloss of choice and cutting,
a lying down toward the wind,
the heaving you were warned about.

And, soon, there is love like
miniature spellings embedded in the shoulder,
waiting to be misspelled, washed,
brought back by perception that fades
with what moves below the arm,
hinging on a doubt cried away.
There is the mistake of giving name
to the prune, the print bitten off
and covered over by black hair—
its numbers kept secret,
long strands in the tale of the carpet,
the pomegranate, the hundred ways
of staying there.

And, besides, there is danger of riding desire
until it carves you into its swollen throat,
steel-cry of possession and the infinite blessing
of fingers missing from the first time,
fingernails tracing the shape of the strawberry
to memorize roughness without leaving.
There is the flavor and the understanding,
a place to rest the eye after traveling,
a force that binds you together
without you knowing red marks
on your back are places where wings
would have risen if you were an angel.

Calling Ourselves

On the lips of the wind, I shall be called a tree
of many birds.
                                    —Rosario Castellanos

As if to gather time like a clock we love to confuse,
we stretch our limbs too far and touch the world
once more without caring who it is we condemn.

The tired man bringing home a small check,
a young girl wishing she was dead,
two lovers confused as to why they cried.

On the eye of the shattered star,
we call ourselves home and wish
those colors we saw were true flight
above vegetation where we hid our desire

to be a second person, or a large box,
an apple, or a startled hawk surprised
(for the first time) its heavy prey fights back.

                         *

This is how we laugh at the knife kissing the heart,
the young boy undressing the teenage girl for the first time,
the parrot in the cage answering the moans in the other room,
cars in traffic turning to nightmares of streets abandoned

in the hour of love when we start laughing
and labor for the anxious lovers who promised
they would rise naked to welcome a third person
in trouble, knocking at their door.

                         *

Of the follower, we know little.
Of the time when we could read old letters
without crying, we forgive little.

Of the animals in our dreams,
we kill many and wake up bloodied,
startled like the flash against bone,
the roar of breath upon our exposed heads,
the nightmare becoming a herd of thin horses
galloping in crooked circles.

Of the concept of falling toward mountains,
we fall beyond clouds more troublesome
than any dumb daydream,

awakening with our blankets on fire,
hurtling ourselves toward a soft touching
of bare feet on cold floors.

*

In the soliloquy of the moon,
a man and a woman exchange bits of fingernails
with tiny love manuscripts painted on before
they clipped them off with their teeth.

*

In the fist of distance
that invites us to dance,

a kidnapped lover waits for the lights
to come on so she can confess.

In the tree of history we can't name,
a crippled angel, thrown from the clouds,

hangs and dies,
lives, then dies.

In the first game invented after
the concept of winning,

a father whispers to his son to beware
the beauty of coming in last.

*

To say farewell with a handshake
that goes beyond touch,
so the good-bye becomes daylight
and the hello comes at night.

It burns in the sweat of bone,
glows when the hand is alone
to mimic hands of friends, lovers,
parents who waved long ago.

It is the last light because the hand
does not hold on for long.
Fingers ignite into torches radiating
want and desire for long fingernails,

cracking knuckles, long life lines in the palms,
applause for how simple it is
to douse handlight by holding on
to someone else's hand.

The Skin Brown

There is no beauty in the alphabet that grows on the face.
How can you say that when the telephone never rings?

One or two pairs of bikini panties thrown on the bed.
There is a mirror where I saw how old I was going to get.

When we decide we have never met a prophet, we are quiet.
When the arroyo rises into view, we wake on marble floors.

When our sisters are being herded down the stairs,
it takes up the rest of our lives.

The word *Lord* belonged in the first poem I wrote.
I had no idea it was in the wrong book.

The roof of my house was a place poverty never reached.
I made a visit to the attic where I found the mushrooms.

I have no rival.
My brother died in the other world.

Look at these things made fast.
They are blankets with hidden symbols woven into them.

The dead bird is my father refusing to answer the phone.
My anger is so clear, it is the whistle of the locomotive.

I was bound to lie about my nightmares.
I was going to tell the truth about my dreams.

The cross gone.
The willow tree in my mother's yard cut down.

I cried under it.
It rained green for days, weeks, even years of standing there.

I am not willing to release my intentions.
I am too tired.

The lightning striking around me as I ran down the dirt street.
A little boy thinking the wall of shame was about to come down.

Some say it is nothing.
Some observe the tracing of names on the stone calendar.

What was my ailment?
Was it not being given a middle name?

I can't describe the lines on the statue of La Virgen de Guadalupe.
The figure has too many moments.

Walking into the gallery, I heard the orange bells.
The '56 Chevy in the junkyard, the barrio razed for a freeway.

When I finally demand a different softness in my mother's ear,
her wrinkled skin is the flower that cast pollen on her pillow.

The skin brown.
Oranges tinged with cool smells of summer.

The skin brown.
Red Kool-Aid made from cold water in the refrigerator.

The skin burned brown.
Hiding under the bed, my father's belt smoking the air, not finding me.

The skin grown red.
No one will leave me alone.

The skin with dozens of black moles.
Once, I guessed they were a riddle.

The skin with white hair and the scar of decades ago.
Once, I hurt my shoulder to wake my body.

The skin brown.
A pale view of the mountains on the tongue.

The skin brown.
To shower in the mud removes every color.

The skin brown and old.
When I was thin as a boy, I kept falling and passing out.

The skin brown and its language.
Whether you live here or there, the blind brown teacher loves you.

"People Born in September Are *Sabio* (Wise) like a *Tecolote* (Owl)"

Howling flame hiding under the plow,
given sacrament to appease the owl.
Claw-written question subdued in the imagination
where concrete targets are temporary
to the angel who benefits from doubt.

Born in September, I kneel
with the rice gone,
distinctions faltering with age and exclusion.
Tapping my stick to wholeness,
no one believes me when I turn
forty-six beyond the mountain.

Howling solid curl of relayed elements
drifting into the bone, food
to be ground into clay plates
left behind,
forgiven to bring back
the bluebird with no name,
who dwells for how well
I was taught to mark my day,

forcing meaning out of wisdom,
falling short of retrieval and peace,
as if outside noise of the younger
displaces each lesson taught in the flower,
each green cut in the ocotillo chasing
secrets going thirsty to reach
the next wet century.

My Mother's Angel

My mother's angel has not forgiven her.
My mother's angel weeps for her
each time her children are made to feel
guilty over their father's betrayal.

My mother's angel hides in a pot of beans,
but she doesn't cook anymore.
She has given up the kitchen,
has no one left to feed.

My mother's angel has not forgiven her
for lying next to her father
on his deathbed, watching
the blood flow out of his mouth.

My mother's angel is a Yaqui avenger
cast out of northern Mexico because
too many dark wings inhabit the arroyos,
kill the people, eat the women,

and tie the men to stone slabs,
forcing old women to say new chants,
superstitions, fears of two-headed *santos*
coming to take their sons away.

My mother's angel has not forgiven her
for shouldering the blame,
taking her children into the church
without teaching them to pray.

My mother's angel can't speak English,
or Spanish, makes the sounds
of the *curandero* who burns onions,
carves cow brains,

smashes rattlesnake meat
into the flour of the palms,
the anointed feet of the field-worker,
strong arms of the bricklayer.

My mother's angel has not forgiven her
and is leaving, taking her children
away from her, giving her one chance
to rise from her father's deathbed
as a small girl who had no choice.

She had to keep photos of him,
the secrets of the desert.
She drove the avenger away
with the weight of her rosary,

the burden of crossing
and recrossing the rooms
of the death house, before the sun
of Arizona turned into
red stone of the first church.

⁓

Angelo

Angelo arrives. I see him stepping through
the flames of my grandfather's whiskers,
taking his place among the silent men of my home,
opening his face to show me the scar—
Angelo without shame or the idea of thirst.

Angelo drops down. I hear him reciting
the chant that killed our father in the war,
moving his mouth as if Mexican hatred
is the same as the oil rubbed on his back
by the biting slave who healed him to life.

Angelo settles in. I listen as he repeats
the order of the birds, wings he tore off
those that were the wrong color of faith,
animals that fed him, made him a legend
among the men who survived to follow.

Angelo leaves. I watch him step into my heart
as if I had room for him and could forgive him
for never speaking, treating me like a mute
brother who wanted to say, "Angelo! Angelo!
Where is your blood? Should I let you,
or should I be ashamed?"

The Head of Pancho Villa

The rumor persisted that the head of Pancho Villa
disappeared on its own before they buried him,
found its way across the Chihuahua desert to El Paso,
where he killed several men and kept women.
The head floated across the Rio Grande,
snapping turtles diving out of its way,
the brown mass moving on its own, his thick hair
and mustache shining in the green water.

The skull of the general evaporated in the heat,
only to reappear at the church door,
the early man who came to pray startled by
the bullet holes between the closed eyes.
He stared at the head, then ran.
When he brought the sleepy Padre to look,
they only found a wet spot on the ground
before they bowed and crossed themselves.

The rumor ran that the head became
the mountain surrounding the town.
Others said it was the skull that sat for years
on the highway west to Arizona.
It was true because my grandparents lived there,
told their children the skull glowed
on the roads, until my grandfather died
and his family returned to the other mountain.

I see the head of Villa each time I drive into El Paso.
It rises off the setting sun as the evening turns red.
By now, I am convinced the eyes are open, the hair longer.
After all, the moon is enough when I turn and take a look.

Forgiveness

Look at how you reach for things already inhabited—
    formed by the ivory face of gregarious shadow,
how you spin what is written in the sky as consequence—
    molded passage entwined in the murmuring hallway
where you understand the common objects—
    pelicans unfolding massive white wings, geese disappearing
above clouded fields, the lone deer entering your yard in trouble,
    one lone coyote running the opposite direction of image—
how you must have seen these things and waited and thought.

Look at part of the flower without asking what happened—
    calcium appearing to ward off the worm and the seed,
how the day weighs its dawn of indifference and calls you—
    there must be several ways to move toward the corner.
Blending the whistle with the carved tooth of a dog, the wineglass,
    a painting of the charging horses with Sioux warriors
screaming at the soldiers to stop running so they can kill them—
    the place where you must have dreamed of revenge,
skies following the river past the outstretched men of sleep.
    There is a purpose here—a flute being dismantled and packed,
lips of the blower calling you to listen to her questions—
    What shall we do with the day?
Who will cross into the idling car and go to sleep?
    How can you love the image of the quiet priests when
they tortured you with candy and the steaming crucifix?

Look at what you have told the hushed crowd—
    how it sinks and waits for the end of disbelief.
There must be a way to say this and keep the flower.
    There must be time to measure the spiderweb and the kiss.
Someone will have left you a message by now—
    Its words emerge from the startled field of jars:
Hurry. Hurry. Be lost and caught and safe and careful.
    When the message is pronounced, you answer.

When you look at what stays, you are serene,
	a replica of measure kneeling down to fold
your hands together on the black floor.

At the Rio Grande near the End of the Century

See how the cottonwood bends at the waist.
    It turns gray, cracking as the sun goes down.
There is no limit to returning.
    See the trunk turn toward what has changed you.

When you place yourself against the river you can't reach,
    it is an old habit draining your hands of strength.
Look at the cottonwood disappearing.
    Its hidden sediment is alighting out of your reach.

It is not water.
    It was not made to mark the border with leaves.
Only the river can cease its mud and turn its brown heart.
    Only the passage belongs to swollen, bare feet.

What you know is the scent of the desert you are so tired
    of writing about,
how it covers the past and hangs as the ember of thought—
    wisdom molded out of the falling world.

What you love is removed from the pale circle of shadows.
    It will never return. It will weep.
Even the moisture in the armpit smells like the trees.
    Tomorrow you will see another kind of growth.

See the threads of the hills turning back the revolt.
    See how the men are crossing the river toward you.
When the cottonwood petrifies in the lone spot,
    history will be overlooked and you will die.

What you keep are the thousand miles of the wounded breast.
    What you smell is the fine cotton of the dying tree.
When the white balls stick to your hair, listen to the fleeing men.
    Even their backs are wet and some of them look like you.

Unraveling in Black

I carry an extra black bead in my pocket.
It broke off a rosary long ago.
I call it *tambora*, timbale,
tin-loud sound of a hard, black ball
that changed the tip of my fingers.

No one wants to notice.
They think I know the truth.
They ask me for tales,
made-up superstitions to frighten
their children and kill wild animals.
Once, I was the hunter feeding the house.

Today, my pockets are empty of riddles,
a few cracked sunflower seeds hidden there,
strings from the lining of my pockets
unraveling in the most unusual way.

In Chicago, I got off the subway,
climbed up the smelly stairs to run into
a young, bald kid who stared at me,
his striped T-shirt caked in dry blood.
I made it to my hotel,
but saw many things in the rain.
One of them was a man who looked
like my father standing on the corner,
watching strangers get off the train.

So many years filled with whispers—
Abuelita, Weli, Tía, Tío,
Vamos a la tienda.
Can I take you to the grocery store?
Shadows and lampshades where my grandmother
used to live with her sister.
Now, my grandmother lives with my mother.

I can't visit because the skinned animal I carved
in my chest is starting to move, inventing whispers,
wanting me to open my ribs, so it can be freed.

The animal in my chest will let me live
if I can answer the riddle of the desert hills,
the hidden men in the subway,
old cars rusting in the dirt,
car tires hiding great mounds of ants,
tumbleweeds covering the spot where I buried
my toy soldiers, never to dig them up again.

Acrylic zigzags.
Cow horns with stranger carvings.
A mask of the priest who dropped of a heart attack.
A piece of hair from the janitor who cleaned the church.
Vigilante Spanish social workers coming to unravel
the puzzle of the streets, meeting their deaths.

Charcoal arms and legs.
One of the first drawings I ever did, where
the huge face of a black man is reciting a song
for the empty chamber where three boys sit
in the endless rows of empty seats,
stare at the black man who grows larger
than a giant as he moans, flies, then comes
down on the altar to scare the boys—
a charcoal drawing I can't explain,
yet recall, but threw away years ago.
A dance of devils wanting to convert choirboys
before the first time they masturbate.

A mean uncle demanding I say the word for frog in Spanish.
My father's father insisting I say *"ratonsito"*—little mouse,
all of them laughing when we visit, none of them
knowing the rotting corpse was in the basement
painting landscapes on their walls.

Juan said, *"All the electric guitars moan in the pawnshops,"*
and I knew what he meant.
A cord, a strap, a string, a stack of broken vinyl 45s.
My mother catching me in my room with my pants down,
six years old, comparing cocks with the boy next door,
little saviors made to feel shame at what they had,
my mother trapping me in the bathroom
as if the show-and-tell was dirty, as if the men
who crossed themselves had no reason to undress
and penetrate the night with the fresh scents
of avocado, *tripas, queso*—
every sauce you could think of smearing
in the ceremony of boys becoming men.

The King of Desire trembles.
He is my imaginary companion.
I speak to him when I am alone.
He tells me stories, teaches me
how to fly without wings, how to leap
off house roofs without breaking,
how to avoid the crazy old man
in the alley with singing knives,
the one who cut Francisco into party pieces,
gave our friend a kiss before painting
his face on the walls of adobe.

The King of Desire has a deck of cards,
an unused condom, a picture of La Virgen,
the key to his brother's footlocker where
the weed sits in bags, a photo of his brother,
lost in Vietnam—the jungles reminding the King
how we dug tunnels under the freeway
when they were still constructing it.
1958—the year Francisco screamed
and left us his sneakers, his mother saying
we could have anything of his we wanted
after the funeral—all we took were his clean,
black high-tops that didn't fit any of us.
They were too big, but we carried the shoes

when we shot hoops at school, set them
on the asphalt for good luck, until
they disappeared in a sudden rainstorm,
the thieves leaving nothing but a torn shoelace
reminding us Francisco shouldn't have
gone to heaven barefoot.

Barefoot.
Bathed.
Naked.
Fat.
Fresh haircut.
No one home.
The rain refusing to stop.
My face in the mirror.
A voice telling me to open the back door,
so the thief can come in.

A voice telling me not to open the house,
so the thief won't escape.

A voice telling me he will get me tonight
when I am asleep.

Did you hear the scream from the basement?
I have never felt so rich in recounting this.

Did you let the black figure come near you?
I have never told you what happened.

Did you say it was cold in the room?
I could not see the open eyes or mouth.

Did the ghost bring his black pit bull with him?
I heard the paws on the floor.

Can you admit what the claw holding down your wrist means?
I am going to live for a very long dream.

Acknowledgments

Many thanks to the editors and publishers of the following journals and anthologies, where some of the poems first appeared.

Alaska Quarterly Review: "Two Striped Lizards";
American Literary Review: "The Cult of the Closed Hand";
American Poetry Review: "Calling Ourselves";
Bitter Oleander: "Breastbone," "From the Face," "The Head of Pancho Villa," "There," "Under the Freeway in El Paso" and "White";
Caliban: "Sentora" and "Llaga";
Denver Quarterly: "The Poor Angel";
El Coro: A Chorus of Latino Poetry (University of Massachusetts Press): "Ese";
Fish Stories: "Under the Freeway in El Paso";
Getting Over the Color Green: Environment and Nature Writing from the Southwest (University of Arizona Press): "The Hawk in the Yard," "The Turtle," and "Two Striped Lizards";
Indiana Review: "Beyond Having";
Kenyon Review: "Explain";
Key Satchel: "Suddenly, I Remember the Place";
Massachusetts Review: "Esé";
Poetry International: "The Angels of Juarez, Mexico";
Railroad Face (Chile Verde Press): "Calling the White Donkey" and "Mexican";
Seneca Review: "Yaqui Poems from Hidden Ancestors";
Touching the Fire: Fifteen Poets of the Latino Renaissance (Anchor/Doubleday): "The Angels of Juárez, Mexico," "At the Rio Grande near the End of the Century," "Beyond Having," "Brown Pot," "Calling the White Donkey," "Still Life with Endings," and "Without Villages";
TriQuarterly: "Angelo" and "Mexican";
Verse: "Still Life with Endings";
Yefief: "Meditation at Chamberino."

My thanks to the San Antonio Commission on the Arts and the Illinois Arts Council for fellowships in poetry, which allowed me to begin and conclude this manuscript. This book would not be possible without the support of my teachers and friends in El Paso, Denver, San Antonio, San Marcos, and Chicago. I will never forget the early encouragement and acceptance of my work by Al Poulin. The voice of poetry was the future.

About the Author

Ray Gonzalez is a poet, essayist, and editor born in El Paso, Texas. He is the author of *Memory Fever: A Journey Beyond El Paso del Norte* (Broken Moon Press, 1993), a memoir about growing up in the Southwest, and *Turtle Pictures* (University of Arizona Press, 2000), a poetic/prose cultural memoir. He was educated at The University of Texas at El Paso and Southwest Texas State University, where he received an MFA in Creative Writing. He is the author of five books of poetry, including *The Heat of Arrivals* (BOA Editions, 1996), which won the 1997 Josephine Miles Book Award for Excellence in Literature. He is the editor of twelve anthologies, most recently *Muy Macho: Latino Men Confront Their Manhood* (1996) and *Touching the Fire: Fifteen Poets of the Latino Renaissance* (1998), both from Anchor/Doubleday Books. He has served as Poetry Editor of *The Bloomsbury Review*, a book review magazine in Denver, for seventeen years. Among his awards are a 1998 Fellowship in Poetry from the Illinois Arts Council, a 1993 Before Columbus Foundation American Book Award for Excellence in Editing, and a 1988 Colorado Governor's Award for Excellence in the Arts. He has taught at the University of Illinois in Chicago and is now an assistant professor of English at the University of Minnesota in Minneapolis.

BOA EDITIONS, LTD.
AMERICAN POETS CONTINUUM SERIES